For my father and in memory of my grandpa Joe, who also served.
—EM

Copyright © 2023 by Erin McGill

Cover design by Kelley Lanuto

Cover and internal design © 2023 by Sourcebooks

Sourcebooks and the colophon are registered trademarks of Sourcebooks.

All rights reserved.

The art was created using cut paper, fabric, ink, watercolor, pastel, gouache, and colored pencil.

Published by Sourcebooks eXplore, an imprint of Sourcebooks Kids

P.O. Box 4410, Naperville, Illinois 60567-4410

(630) 961-3900

sourcebookskids.com

Cataloging-in-Publication Data is on file with the Library of Congress.

Source of Production: PrintPlus Limited, Shenzhen, Guangdong Province, China

Date of Production: January 2023

Run Number: 5029232

Printed and bound in China.

PP 10 9 8 7 6 5 4 3 2 1

We Also Served

Served

True Stories of
Brave Animals
in the Military
& other heroic tales

by Erin McGill

sourcebooks
eXplore

We animals are the unsung heroes of conflict and war.

Gallantly, we leave our loved ones, and we put ourselves in harm's way. We are brave and loyal. We show perseverance and strength. We enlist, get drafted, and volunteer. Even in the bleakest times of war, we give companionship and strength.

With our wings, whiskers, paws, hooves, or even our light,
we also served. These are our stories.

Sergeant Stubby, WWI

Mascot Dog

I was found wandering around the campus of Yale University, homeless and hungry. Soldiers were training there and getting ready to ship out. They saw me, gave me some scraps to eat, and petted me. I wanted to earn my keep, so I learned to march and salute like them.

Corporal Robert Conroy and his mates gave me my name and made me the official mascot of the 102nd Infantry Regiment. When we left America for the war, I served as a sentry alongside my two-legged brothers. In the trenches in France, they took care of me and I took care of them. They thanked me for my service with a uniform decorated with many medals and gave me an honorary rank.

With loyalty, I also served.

Medals given by soldiers

Rank: Sergeant

Wound Chevron

1914–1918
Commemorative War
Medal from France

Battle of
Verdun Medal

Purple Heart

Old Abe, American Civil War

Mascot Eagle

I was separated from my family when I was just an eaglet and given to the Eighth Wisconsin Infantry to be its mascot. I proudly perched on a stand especially built for me to lead our troops. A captain named me Old Abe after our President Abraham Lincoln. My infantry was named the Eagle Regiment in my honor, now known as the 101st Airborne Division.

The Battle of Farmington, Mississippi, was my first time in combat. The soldiers were ordered to lie low. At first, I was not allowed to join them for fear of alerting the enemy. But that was not going to stop me! I flattened my wings and lay quietly beside them until it was safe.

After I retired from service, the funds from the sales of my photographs and the feathers I shed went to help my fellow sick and disabled soldiers.

With empathy, I also served.

Rip, WWII

Search and Rescue Dog

I was a scruffy mutt living on the streets of London. After an attack in 1940, an air raid warden named E. King took me in. I was forever grateful and wanted to show my thanks. With my keen nose and sharp hearing, I tore into action. I helped find people trapped in the rubble. They were so relieved to see me and get a lick when I located them. I became one of the first-ever search and rescue dogs employed in war, eventually saving over one hundred lives.

With faithfulness, I also served.

Search and Rescue Dog

My owner Mr. Barnett and his team were summoned to dig out debris after a night of heavy bombing in London. I picked up a scent and split off from the others. The team saw me digging furiously at the rubble. They helped me move away layers of bricks, and we discovered a cat submerged under a table. My new feline friend became the first of sixty-three animals I saved during the war. Like Rip, I became another one of the first search and rescue dogs. Many people lost their homes and businesses during the war and feared the loss of their beloved pets. Whether they had fur or fins, I was determined to find them.

With proficiency, I also served.

Sergeant Reckless, Korean War

Military Horse

I joined the Marines to haul ammunition to the front lines. I became very close with my comrades on and off the battlefield. During a five-day battle, I made fifty-one trips climbing through steep mountain trails and trudging through rice paddies. I carried almost five tons all by myself. If I saw a wounded soldier, I would give him a lift as well. In battles, I tried to shield my fellow soldiers with my body. I was wounded twice. The soldiers were so grateful that in return they threw their jackets over me, putting themselves in danger.

This got me a promotion. I was the only hoofed sergeant. By the time the war ended, I was awarded numerous honors, including two Purple Hearts, two presidential unit citations, several service medals, and the Marine Corps Good Conduct Medal.

With strength, I also served.

United Nations Korea Medal

Korean Service Medal

Marine Corps Good Conduct Medal

National Defense Service Medal

Navy Unit Commendation

Purple Heart

Rank: Staff Sergeant

Army Presidential Unit Citation

Republic of Korea Presidential Unit Citation

French Fourragère

Animals in War and Peace Medal of Bravery

PDSA Dickin Medal

Smoky, WWII

Therapy Dog

In the jungles of New Guinea, Corporal William A. Wynne was looking for a dog, and I was looking for a friend. I followed him everywhere. Wynne knew a lot about dog training, so he taught me many tricks to entertain the troops, and I was eager to please. Barrel rolling, tightrope walking, even spelling my name in colored blocks, my tricks brought the troops great joy.

My training came in handy when Wynne contracted dengue fever. I was able to visit him at the hospital. The nurses saw how happy I made Wynne, so they began to take me on rounds to visit the other wounded and sick soldiers. The soldiers loved me because they knew I was one of them. I visited many hospitals during and after the war to bring soldiers comfort, becoming the first therapy dog.

With heart, I also served.

Cher Ami, WWI

Homing Pigeon

In the service of the U.S. Army Signal Pigeon Corps, I flew twelve successful missions throughout the war and returned unharmed. My last assignment would be different. Over five hundred of my men were in danger and we needed reinforcements. It was left to three of us pigeons to get the message to headquarters. The others took off first, but the enemy quickly brought them down. Everyone was now relying on me. The enemy got me too. My mates watched the sky, waiting for me to fall, but I did not. My chest, leg, and eye were badly injured, yet I made it back to headquarters. Without me, very few of us would have made it. When I was nursed back to health, the French government presented me with a very prestigious medal of honor that no other animal had ever received.

With bravery, I also served.

**Animals in War and Peace
Medal of Bravery**

Croix De Guerre

Nemo, Vietnam War

Dog Soldier

I was one of the first dogs shipped off to serve in this war. My handler and I patrolled the perimeter of our base. We were the first line of defense. When our base was attacked, I leapt into action, giving my handler, Airman Robert Throneburg, a chance to radio for help. I shielded him with my body until help arrived.

Our teamwork helped us survive the battle. I received a hero's welcome back home and went on to become a recruitment dog, encouraging dog owners to enlist their dogs.

With fortitude, I also served.

Nemo A534
Oct 1962 - Dec. 1972

Department of the Air Force

Simon, Chinese Civil War

Mascot Cat

I was seen scrounging around the docks in search of a bite to eat when a sailor spotted me. The seaman thought I was just what his ship needed and took me aboard as the mascot of the HMS *Amethyst*. After all, we cats have a variety of uses on ships, and feline friends have accompanied sailors since ancient times.

My ship was sent into dangerous territory during the Chinese Civil War. We flew a white flag to show our neutrality, but it didn't matter. We were hit more than fifty times. Many ships tried to come to our rescue, but they were also hit. While we waited in a standoff for months, rats got into our food rations. They posed a real danger to the health of everyone onboard.

Food was scarce. The crew needed me to vanquish the rat army. I was triumphant! For my victory, I was promoted to able seaman. No one thought a small stray cat could survive a blast and then muster up the strength to rid the *Amethyst* of pestilence and vermin. I became the first and only feline to receive the Dickin Medal for displays of bravery in battle.

With tenacity, I also served.

Judy, WWII

Mascot Dog and Prisoner of War

I was originally a mascot for the HMS *Grasshopper*. My ship was destroyed in a bombing raid in Indonesia. Some of the crew and I managed to swim to shore. We were stranded until a Chinese boat picked us up and brought us to another island, but before we could reach safety, we were surrounded by Japanese troops. We were captured and became prisoners of war. I wasn't given any rations like the other registered soldiers, but thankfully Airman Frank Williams kindly saved me a few scraps. Since I wasn't registered like the other prisoners, no one outside of the camp knew I existed and I had no rights. Williams again came to my rescue. I was registered as POW 81A and became the only animal ever to be a POW. Williams and I were inseparable.

After we were finally released from the camp, our boat was struck by a torpedo, became engulfed in flames, and started sinking. Williams pushed me out of a hole below deck. We both feared we had lost each other. Other soldiers needed me, so I paddled back and forth, shuttling them to shore. We were soon reunited, but were not in the clear yet as we were POWs again and many of our captors did not want me to be there. Williams always had a plan and I was always eager to follow. When Williams sensed danger, he would yell, "Scramble!" and I would scurry off into the jungle and hide, sometimes waiting days for his call back that it was safe. He always called and I always returned.

With reverence, I also served.

PDSA Dickin Medal

Lucca, Iraq and Afghanistan Wars

Bomb-Sniffing Dog

I used my keen sense of smell to sniff out bombs for the U.S. Marine Corps. During my four hundred missions over six years of service, there was not a single casualty. On my very last mission, I discovered an improvised explosive device in a field. I got injured while protecting my platoon. My fellow marines knew how many times I had saved them. It was their turn to help me. They nursed me back to health. When I retired and returned home, I wanted the world to know what important work we animals do. I became an ambassador visiting wounded warriors and schools.

With devotion, I also served.

Salty and Roselle, 9/11

Guide Dogs

We were guide dogs for the visually impaired. We went to work each day with our owners, Omar Rivera and Michael Hingson, at the World Trade Center in New York City.

We sat quietly under their desks each day until September 11, 2001, when a plane struck the building where our owners worked. Neither of us were trained military dogs, but we were guide dogs. We knew how to stay calm by our owners' side. Smoke engulfed the building. Debris was plunging. So many of those around us felt helpless, but we used our keen sense of smell to help the people around us descend the many flights of stairs down to safety.

With companionship, we also served.

PDSA Dickin Medals

All of us animals courageously did our bit. But some of our human counterparts did not think that we deserved the honor or even healthcare that two-legged soldiers received. Many of us walked the streets unappreciated, without the support or good care we deserved.

One person did take notice: Maria Dickin. She wanted to honor those animals who were not allowed to receive commendations such as the Medal of Honor or the Victoria Cross. In 1943, the first Dickin Medal was awarded. On the medal there is a laurel wreath, signifying triumph. To this day, it continues to be presented to us unsung heroes of war.

For gallantry, we also served.

Four-Pawed Soldiers

The History of Dog Combat

Dogs have helped in wars for centuries. They've trained in combat to be used as scouts, sentries, messengers, mercy dogs, and trackers. In ancient times, Roman general Julius Caesar trained large Celtic mastiffs to fight in battle. The mastiff breed was also used by Spanish Conquistadors because the dogs are so large that they often frightened their opponents. In modern wars such as in Afghanistan and Iraq, the U.S. military relied heavily on military working dogs and their handlers to sniff out concealed bombs and other weapons, as well as alerting their handlers to hidden soldiers. Fun fact: Many military working dogs that served in Iraq and Afghanistan wear goggles specially made for dogs to protect their eyes from dust and debris when helicopters take off.

Dogs for Defense

The U.S. military used few dogs during WWI, but French and German armies used thousands. As America entered WWII, it realized the value of war dogs. The military asked citizens to volunteer their dogs to serve. The American people donated thousands of dogs to Dogs for Defense, many of them beloved family pets. The dogs learned to be sentries, scouts, messengers, and mine detectives.

Robby's Law

Dogs continued to be deployed during the Korean and Vietnam Wars, and although soldiers formed strong bonds with their canine companions, they were forced to leave them behind. The military feared that the dogs could not be retrained for civilian life and that it was too expensive to bring them home. Veteran dog handlers lobbied for change. In 2000, Congress and former President Bill Clinton approved a bill called "Robby's Law," allowing veteran U.S. military working dogs (MWDs) to be adopted. An amendment was added to the bill in 2016 by President Barack Obama that guaranteed the safe return of *all* retired military dogs after serving abroad, including their medical care. Many MWDs now get to return home with their handlers and help veterans with their PTSD.

In the Sky and On the Ground

Feathered Fighters

Pigeons have been dedicated and reliable messengers for humans for thousands of years. They have a natural homing ability, always returning to their home base after a flight, even when they are released from very far away or unfamiliar surroundings. Ancient Egyptians, Greeks, and Romans all used pigeons to communicate. During WWI and

WWII, over half a million pigeons served. Many pigeons faced extreme adverse conditions. Like most birds, pigeons do not see well at night and do not like to fly over water. Many pigeons flew through extreme weather conditions in the dark over large bodies of water. Pigeons had various duties including aerial survey work, and some were outfitted with a small camera before flying a mission. They also served in many airborne missions, including paratroopers.

The United States Army Pigeon Service, also known as Signal Pigeon Corps, was a unit of the U.S. Army during WWI and WWII. They trained and used homing pigeons for communication and reconnaissance purposes. Many people that kept racing pigeons were asked to donate their birds for the war effort. During WWII, the USAPS consisted of 3,150 soldiers and 54,000 war pigeons. The pigeons were considered an undetectable method of communication. Over 90% of the messages they sent were received. More lives were saved because of pigeons in WWI and WWII than any other animal. The U.S. Army discontinued using pigeons in 1957.

Hoofed Heroes

Horses can be shy, high-strung, and can startle easily, but their speed, loyalty, and willingness to work have made them important assets in times of war. In the United States, horses had important roles in both the Revolutionary War and the Civil War. In the Revolutionary War, General George Washington—later the nation's first president—saw how important horses were and recommended establishing the Calvary Corps. During the American Civil War, horses and mules were extremely important in the transport of artillery as well as soldiers from each battle site.

The invention of the automobile in the early twentieth century transformed transportation, but during WWI, there was still a need for horses, especially on rough terrain where it was difficult for early automobiles to navigate. The animals carried food, ammunition, medicine, and other supplies to soldiers in the trenches. They also served as ambulances, carrying wounded soldiers to help. These horses, as well as mules, endured extreme weather conditions and scarcity of food, many surviving on soggy oats when there was little else to eat.

The need for horses and mules during WWII dramatically decreased due to the improvement of automobiles. But they were used on rugged terrain in North Africa, Italy, and in the China-Burma-India campaign. Mules became preferred over horses because they were more sure-footed, less flighty, hardier, and could survive on fewer rations.

More Brave Animals

While dogs, cats, birds, horses, and mules are the most well-known military animals, many others have served throughout history. Did you know that the British military drafts goats as mascots? The tradition began during the Revolutionary War when a goat wandered onto the battlefield and ended up parading with the British regiment. When the British won the battle, they considered the goat a good omen, thus starting the tradition and a goat has been present ever since.

Elephants and camels have been used as both beasts of burden and a mode of transportation. Elephants are rarely used in conflicts today, but during WWII, they were used to haul heavy artillery and help transport soldiers in Asia. Camels were used for the same purposes and served in WWI, especially in battles in Africa and the Middle East. The British even created the Imperial Camel Corps in 1916 for desert battles.

In the dark, murky trenches of WWI, soldiers found illumination from glowworms. It only took a few glowworms to provide enough light at night for officers to study battle maps and plans, or for soldiers to write letters home or for pigeoneers to write messages for their birds to carry the next day.

In 1959, the U.S. Navy started the U.S. Navy Mammal Marine Program as a way to improve the design of torpedoes and submarines by studying how dolphins moved in the water. Researchers soon realized that the animals had a range of very desirable skills. Dolphins can locate objects quickly with echolocation, which is a form of sonar. Sea lions were also studied, and researchers learned they have excellent vision and are very good at spotting lost objects underwater. Today the mammal program trains bottlenose dolphins and California sea lions to find and retrieve equipment lost in the ocean. The animals are also taught to survey underwater sites by trainers attaching cameras to their fins.

Land mines, which are explosive devices concealed underground, can remain dangerous many years after a war or conflict has ended, often putting civilians at risk. In recent years, rats have come to the rescue! Gambian pouched rats, which can grow to be the size of a cat, possess a very keen sense of smell and can learn to detect land mines. A Gambian pouched rat named Magawa sniffed out seventy-one land mines and dozens more explosive items in Cambodia over his five-year career. He was the first animal outside of a dog to receive the PDSA Gold Medal, which is the civilian equivalent of the Dickin Medal.